Catholic Churches

Clare Richards

First published in Great Britain by Heinemann Library
Halley Court, Jordan Hill, Oxford OX2 8EJ
a division of Reed Educational and Professional Publishing Ltd.
Heinemann is a registered trademark of Reed Educational & Professional Publishing Limited.

OXFORD MELBOURNE AUCKLAND
JOHANNESBURG IBADAN BLANTYRE GABORONE
PORTSMOUTH NH (USA) CHICAGO

Designed by Tinstar Design (www.tinstar.co.uk)
Printed by South China Printing in Hong Kong / China

04 03 02 01 00
10 9 8 7 6 5 4 3 2 1

British Library Cataloguing in Publication Data

Richards, Clare
    Catholic churches. - (Places of worship)
    1. Catholic church buildings - Juvenile literature
    I. Title
    246.9'582

ISBN 0 431 05192 5
This title is also available in a hardback library edition (ISBN 0 431 05187 9)

Acknowledgements

The Publishers would like to thank the following for permission to reproduce photographs:
Andes Press Agency/Carlos-Reyes Manzo, pp. 4, 5, 6, 7, 8, 9, 10, 11, 12, 13 (left), 14, 15, 16, 17,
18, 19, 20, 21; Circa Photo Library, p.13 (right).

Cover photograph of St Joseph's Catholic church, Sale, reproduced with permission of
J. Allan Cash.

Our thanks to Philip Emmett for his comments in the preparation of this book, and to Louise
Spilsbury for all her hard work.

Every effort has been made to contact copyright holders of any material reproduced in this
book. Any omissions will be rectified in subsequent printings if notice is given to the Publisher.

Contents

Words printed in **bold letters like these**
are explained in the Glossary.

What is a Catholic church?

A church is a building where **Christians** meet to **worship**. Christians are people who learn about **God** by following the teaching of his son, **Jesus**.

Some Christians are called **Roman Catholics** because their leader lives in Rome. He is called the **Pope**.

The Catholic Cathedral of Christ, the King, Liverpool, England.

What do churches look like?

Catholic churches are different shapes and sizes. Some are very old buildings and others are new.

A few of the largest churches are called cathedrals, and small church buildings are often called chapels.

The Slipper Chapel in Walsingham, England.

Looking outside the church

Roman Catholic churches are all different, but many are built in the shape of a cross or rectangle. Some modern ones are round.

The cross is an important **symbol** for **Christians**. They believe that **Jesus** was killed by being fastened to a cross. This is called **crucifixion**.

Can you see the cross on this church?

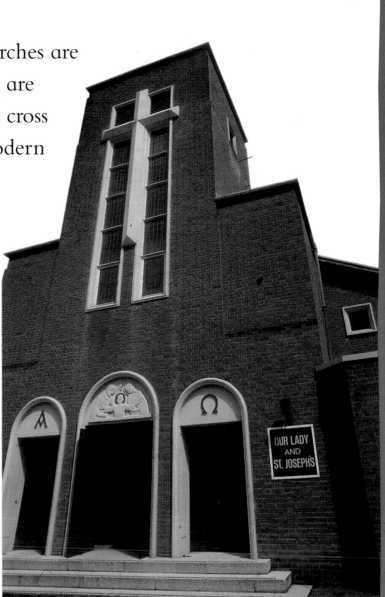

OUR LADY
AND
ST. JOSEPH'S

Statues

If you look outside a Roman Catholic church you may be able to see a **crucifix** or statue. Sometimes the statue is of **Mary**, who is important to Catholics because she was the mother of Jesus.

There may be a statue of a **saint**. Saints are Christians who tried really hard to follow Jesus's teachings. People learn from their good example. Churches are often named after a saint. Look out for statues and crucifixes inside the church too.

This statue is of Our Lady, a name Catholics give to Mary.

What's inside?

Some new churches are simple inside, but many of the older churches are richly decorated.

When **Catholics** go into church, they make a **sign of the cross** with **holy** water from a special bowl near the door. First they touch their forehead, then their chest and then both shoulders to make a cross shape.

People sit on chairs or special benches called pews. These are usually in rows, facing the front of the church, where the **altar** is.

Inside a church, with a **service** going on.

Church pictures

Some churches have stained glass windows. These make the church look beautiful and some tell stories from the **Bible**.

In all Catholic churches you can see pictures around the walls called Stations of the Cross. They show the places **Jesus** stopped on the last, sad journey to his death.

One of the Stations of the Cross, pictures on the walls found in all Catholic churches.

Things to look for

When you go into a church, see if you can find the **altar**. It stands in an open space called the **sanctuary**. The altar is usually covered with a cloth.

At the altar the **priest** celebrates **Mass**, the most important **Catholic service**, when he gives out special bread called **Communion**. There is a decorated box called a **tabernacle** near the altar. Communion bread is kept in it to be taken to people who are too ill to come to church.

This altar cloth has a fish **symbol** on it. A fish was used by the first **Christians** as a symbol for **Jesus**. Can you see the tabernacle?

Lecterns

All Catholic churches have a special reading desk, called a lectern. It is usually made of wood and holds a **Bible** or book of prayers. During Mass the **Gospel** is read from the lectern. The Gospel is the part of the Bible that tells the story of Jesus.

Pulpit

The pulpit is a raised platform at the front of the church. It is usually made of wood or stone. The person who leads a service, usually the priest, stands in it to give the **sermon**.

The Gospel is read from the lectern.

Who goes there?

Many **Catholics** meet in church, usually on Sundays. They are greeted by the **priest**, who leads the **worship**. When people gather to pray at a church **service** they are called the **congregation**.

The priest may have an assistant, called a deacon. He is either a man training to be a priest, or sometimes a married man chosen from the congregation.

A priest meeting people outside the church after a service.

Music makers

Music is an important part of worship in church. Most churches have a large musical instrument called an organ. An organ can make lots of different sounds when air is blown through different sized pipes. The organist plays **hymns** which the congregation or **choir** sing during a service.

Sometimes more modern hymns are accompanied by a guitar or other musical instruments.

Singing during a service may be accompanied by an organ (right) or by other instruments, like these violins (below).

Worship in the church

The **Mass** is the most important **service** for **Catholics**. It is celebrated every day in most churches. It is a reminder of the Last Supper (the last meal which **Jesus** shared with his friends), his death on the cross and his rising from the dead (called **resurrection**).

At Mass, prayers are said and **hymns** are sung to praise **God**.

Sunday Mass in a Catholic church.

Communion

The most important part of Mass is the **Communion**. Catholics believe that when they eat and drink the bread and wine **blessed** at Mass they are closer to God.

Communion is given out by the **priest**. He is sometimes helped by people who have volunteered to become **Eucharistic ministers**.

A Eucharistic minister helping to give Communion.

The Eucharist

Communion is also called Eucharist, which means thanksgiving. Jesus gave thanks to God in this way at the Last Supper.

Festivals in the church

Christians celebrate many festivals in church. Easter and Christmas are two of the most important.

Easter

Easter is the celebration of the **resurrection** in spring. Christians believe that after **Jesus** died on the cross, he rose again and now lives among his followers.

At Easter churches are beautifully decorated. On Easter night the Paschal (Easter candle) is lit from a bonfire. This is a **symbol**. It shows that the light of the world (Jesus) has returned.

Lighting the Easter candle.

Christmas

Christmas is a festival to celebrate the birth of Jesus 2000 years ago. At Christmas the church is decorated with Christmas trees, stars and winter greenery. There may also be a model nativity scene, which tells the story of Jesus's birth.

During Advent, the four-week preparation for Christmas, Christians sing joyful **hymns** called carols, which tell the Christmas story.

Cardinal Hume, leader of the Catholic Church in England, with schoolchildren at a carol **service** in Westminster Cathedral.

Special ceremonies

Catholics believe that their lives are a journey to **God**. The most important stages of the journey are celebrated in church as **Sacraments**. Catholics celebrate seven stages on the journey.

The first time Catholics receive **Communion** is a special Sacrament. Children prepare with their families and sometimes at school. They think about the whole **community** and make a promise to be as loving as **Jesus** was to everyone in the community.

Children dress in beautiful clothes on the day they receive their first Communion.

Baptism and confirmation

Catholic parents celebrate the birth of their child with their **Christian** community in church. The baby is welcomed into the church community in a ceremony called **baptism**.

A **minister** baptizes a baby by pouring water from the **font** over the child's head.

When they are old enough to make their own promises to live like Jesus, children repeat the promises made for them by their parents in the baptism ceremony. This special ceremony is called **Confirmation**, and it is celebrated by the **bishop**.

The church and the community

Catholics who meet in church also meet and work together in the wider **community**. Some work together to help people in need. Children may go to the same Catholic school, where they learn and **worship** together. Catholics believe **God** is close to them when they pray and work together in this way.

Catholic schoolchildren involved in a fund-raising activity.

Monks and nuns

Monks and nuns are **Christians** who choose to live in special communities. Both monks (men) and nuns (women) celebrate **Mass** each day and meet several times a day to sing prayers.

Many monks and nuns work as part of the wider community. They may be teachers or they may work with homeless people or others who are in need.

Nun teacher working with children.

Glossary

altar table in church used at Mass

baptism (BAP-tiz-um) ceremony in which a person, usually a baby, becomes a church member

Bible (BY-bull) Christian holy book. The part called the New Testament tells about Jesus's life.

bishop leader of the Church community in a given area

blessed set apart for use in worship (water, candles etc)

cathedral large church at the centre of a Christian community

Catholic see Roman Catholic (page 23)

chapel small place of worship

choir (KWIRE) group of singers

Christian (KRIS-tee-an) someone who follows the religion of Christianity. They believe in God, and they believe that Jesus was God's son.

Communion (kom-YOO-nee-un) when Christians eat bread and drink wine to remember Jesus and his teachings

community (KOM-yoo-nittee) group of people who share the same beliefs and who pray together in the same way

Confirmation service in which people make for themselves the promises that were made for them when they were baptized as babies

congregation group that comes together in church

crucifix (KROO-si-ficks) cross with the figure of Jesus on it

crucifixion (KROO-si-fick-shun) put to death by being fastened to a cross

Eucharist (YOO-ker-ist) thanksgiving, another word for the
  Mass and Communion

font water basin used at baptism

God Christians believe that God made, sees and knows everything

Gospel part of the Bible that tells the story of Jesus

holy means respected because it is to do with God

hymn song written to be sung in church services

Jesus Christians believe that Jesus was the son of God

Mary mother of Jesus

Mass Catholic service of readings, prayers and Communion

minister someone who leads worship and works with people who go to
  church or live nearby. The minister may also be called a priest.

Pope leader of the Catholic Church, who lives in Rome

priest man who leads church services

resurrection (rez-erek-shun) Christian belief that God made Jesus
  alive again

Roman Catholic Christian who accepts the Pope as their leader

Sacraments seven celebrations which bring Jesus into people's lives

saint holy person who lives like Jesus

sanctuary special space in church from which services are led

sermon short talk given to the people, by the priest, at a service

service meeting in church to worship God

sign of the cross gesture with the right hand, touching forehead, chest
  and both shoulders, reminding worshippers of Jesus's death on the cross

symbol sign or object with a special meaning

tabernacle (tab-er-nak-el) precious box in which bread blessed at Mass
  is kept for those who are ill

worship (WUR-ship) show respect and love for God

Index